Memorial Day

Mir Tamim Ansary

Heinemann Library
Des Plaines, Illinois

© 1999 Reed Educational & Professional Publishing
Published by Heinemann Library,
an imprint of Reed Educational & Professional Publishing,
1350 East Touhy Avenue, Suite 240 West
Des Plaines, IL 60018

Printed in Hong Kong / China

03 02 01 00 99
10 9 8 7 6 5 4 3 2 1

Library of Congress Cataloging-in-Publication Data
Ansary, Mir Tamim, 1954-
    Memorial Day / Mir Tamim Ansary.
        p.   cm. — (Holiday histories)
    Includes bibliographical references and index.
    Summary: Introduces Memorial Day, explaining the historical events behind it, how it became a holiday, and how it is observed.
    ISBN 1-57572-874-5 (lib. bdg.)
    1. Memorial Day—Juvenile literature. [1. Memorial Day.
    2. United States—History—Civil War, 1861-1865. 3. Holidays.]
    I. Title. II. Series: Ansary, Mir Tamim. Holiday histories.
    E642.A57   1998
    394.262—dc21   98-14377
                                                                CIP
                                                                AC

Acknowledgments
The publisher would like to thank the following for permission to reproduce photographs:

Cover: UPI/Corbis-Bettmann

Photo Edit/Tony Freeman, p. 5; Stock Boston/John Loletti, p. 6; Magnum Photo/Eugene Richards, p. 7; Super Stock, pp. 8, 10, 15, 19, 26; Photo Researchers, Inc., p. 9(left); The Granger Collection, pp. 9(right), 10, 11, 12, 13, 14, 16(all), 20, 21, 22; John Andress, p 23; Mississippi Department of Archives and History, p. 24(left); Photo Edit/Gary Conner, p. 24; Theater Pix/Michael Brosilow, p.27; *Center Daily Times*, p. 28–29.

Every effort has been made to contact copyright holders of any material reproduced in this book. Any omissions will be rectified in subsequent printings if notice is given to the publisher.

Some words are shown in bold, **like this**. You can find out what they mean by looking in the glossary.

Contents

A Day for Remembering

Memorial Day is the last Monday in May. Flowers are blooming. The school year will be over soon. It's a fine day for outdoor fun.

But there is another side to Memorial Day. This holiday is about remembering. On this day, we remember people who died in wars.

Memorial Day Customs

Many Americans put flags and flowers on graves of people who gave their lives for our country. This family lost a loved one in the Vietnam War. He died in 1970.

This family lost someone in World War Two. They lost him in 1944. They still decorate his grave on Memorial Day. It is an old **custom.**

The Roots of a Holiday

Memorial Day goes back to the Civil War.
That was the biggest war ever fought on
U. S. soil. The Civil War ended in 1865.

8

In the Civil War, Americans fought Americans. Our country had split in two. The North fought the South. The fight was about **slavery.**

A **Union,** or Northern, soldier

A Confederate, or Southern, soldier

Freedom and Slavery

The United States was **founded** as a land of freedom. But there was a problem from the start. Some people in America were **slaves**.

10

Slavery was allowed in the Southern states. The South had big farms. And on those farms, slaves did most of the work.

A Nation Torn

Slavery was against the law in the North.

There, most people felt slavery was wrong.

Many wanted to **ban** it in all states.

Every time a new state joined the country, the question came up. Should slavery be allowed here? Fights broke out over the question.

Civil War

In 1860, the Southern states tried to leave the United States. They said they were a new country. They bombed a U.S. fort.

Abraham Lincoln was president then. He said our country was a **union**. No state had a right to split away. He sent armies to fight the **rebels**.

The Battle of Gettysburg

The South had a great general named Robert E. Lee. Lee drove the **union** armies back. Then he **invaded** the North.

A big battle took place near Gettysburg, Pennsylvania. It lasted three days. More than 43 thousand men died or were hurt. Lee's army was driven south again.

★

Lincoln's Greatest Speech

President Lincoln went to Gettysburg. He gave a speech to **honor** the dead. He explained what the men had died for.

Lincoln said the United States stood for a great idea: Every person is born equal and free. If the country split, he said, this idea would die.

The Tide Turns

After the Battle of Gettsyburg, the North found a great general, too. His name was Ulysses S. Grant. He began wearing down the **rebels**.

At last, Lee gave up. The United States would stay together as one country. And no one in this country would be a **slave**.

*General Robert E. Lee **surrenders** to General Grant, ending the Civil War.*

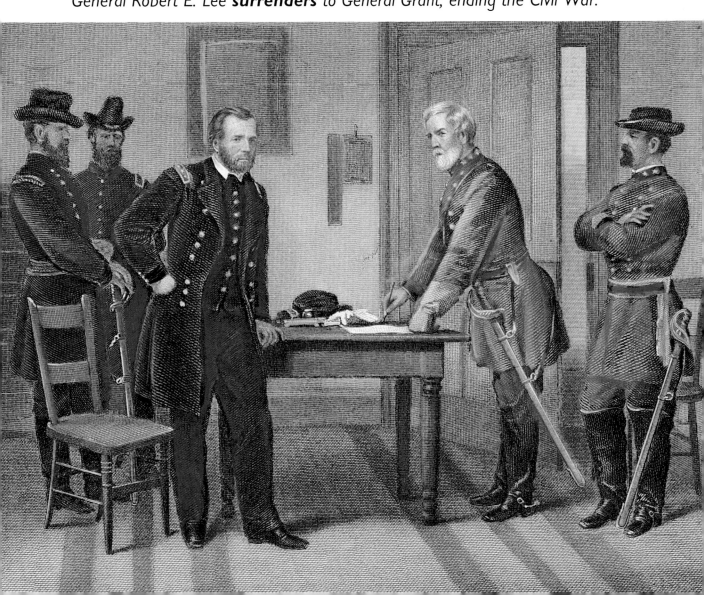

Healing the Wounds

But how could people in the North and South be friends again? The war had left so many people hurt. It had left so much hate.

One day, a group of women went to a
cemetery in Columbus, Mississippi. Soldiers
from both the North and South were buried
there. The women did something wonderful.

Memorial Day Begins

The women put flowers on the soldiers' graves. They didn't ask which side they fought for. They **honored** all the soldiers.

This picture shows the women who helped start Memorial Day.

People in other towns copied this idea. And that is how Memorial Day began. In 1948, it was made into a national holiday.

Memorial Day in Our Time

Memorial Day **honors** all who have died in our country's wars. There is a big **ceremony** at the national cemetery in Arlington, Virginia.

Small ceremonies take place across the country. People put flowers and tiny flags on graves. Some **mourn** in private.

Sadness and Joy

But Memorial Day is not just a sad time. Many towns have festivals on this day. Here is the big festival at Boalburg, Pennsylvania.

Festivals like these mix joy with sadness. They remind us of a good thing on this day in May. Spring and summer always come again.

Important Dates

Memorial Day

1776	The United States is **founded**
1860	South Carolina quits the **Union**
1861	The Civil War begins
1863	Battle of Gettysburg
1864	Ulysses S. Grant takes charge of Union armies
1865	The Civil War ends
1866	Women decorate graves in Columbus, Mississippi
1945	World War Two ends
1948	Memorial Day is declared a national holiday
1975	The Vietnam War ends

Glossary

ban to make something against the law

ceremony special activities to honor someone or something

custom things people always do on special days or for certain events

discover to find something before anyone else

founded set up something new, such as a country

honor to show respect for someone

invaded entered a land or country by force to take over

mourn to feel or show sadness about a loss

rebels those who fight against their government

slaves people who are owned by and work for other people

slavery to use people as slaves

surrenders gives up

union group of many parts that works together; Northern states during the Civil War

More Books to Read

Scott, Geoffrey. *Memorial Day*. Minneapolis, Minn: Lerner Publishing Group, 1983.

Sorensen, Lynda. *Memorial Day*. Vero Beach, Fla: Rourke Press, 1994.

Spies, Karen. *Our National Holidays*. Brookfield, Conn: Millbrook Press, 1992.

Index